Introduction to Social Media Influence

Understanding the Power of Social Media

In this digital era, social media has become an integral part of our lives. It has revolutionized the way we communicate, share information, and connect with others. The power of social media is undeniable, and in this subchapter, we will explore its various aspects and how it can be harnessed for personal and professional growth.

For teenagers, social media has become a significant platform for self-expression and building relationships. It allows them to connect with friends, share their thoughts and experiences, and explore their interests. However, it is essential for teenagers to understand the potential risks and consequences of their online actions. This subchapter will delve into the importance of digital citizenship, online safety, and responsible social media usage. By understanding the power of social media, teenagers can make informed decisions and utilize these platforms positively.

Parents play a crucial role in guiding their children through the digital landscape. They need to be aware of the influence and impact that social media can have on their teenagers' lives. This subchapter will provide insights into monitoring their children's online activities, fostering open communication, and promoting responsible social media usage. By understanding the power of social media, parents can play an active role in ensuring their children's well-being and helping them navigate the digital world safely.

For aspiring YouTubers and influencers, social media is the ultimate tool for building an audience and establishing their personal brand. This subchapter will explore the strategies, tips, and techniques for leveraging social media platforms to enhance visibility, engage with followers, and create meaningful content. It will also shed light on the potential pitfalls and challenges that come with being an influencer, such as dealing with online negativity and maintaining authenticity.

In the niche of fitness and wellness influencers, social media has become a game-changer. It provides a platform to share health and wellness tips, inspire others, and build a community of like-minded individuals. This subchapter will delve into the power of social media in the fitness industry, highlighting the opportunities and responsibilities that come with being a fitness influencer. From creating impactful content to leveraging social media algorithms, this section will equip fitness and wellness influencers with the knowledge and tools they need to thrive in the digital realm.

Understanding the power of social media is essential for teenagers, parents, YouTubers, and fitness and wellness influencers alike. It has the potential to shape our lives, careers, and relationships. By harnessing its power responsibly and strategically, we can create a positive and influential presence in the online world.

The Rise of Influencer Culture

In recent years, a new phenomenon has taken the world by storm: influencer culture. Social media platforms such as Instagram and YouTube have given birth to a new breed of celebrities - influencers. These individuals have managed to amass thousands, if not millions, of followers who hang on their every word and eagerly await their next post.

So, what exactly is an influencer? Simply put, influencers are individuals who have built a strong online presence and have the power to shape the thoughts, opinions, and purchasing decisions of their followers. They have become the go-to source for fashion advice, beauty tips, lifestyle inspiration, and much more. Influencers come in various forms, from beauty gurus to fitness and wellness enthusiasts, and they cater to different niches.

Teenagers, in particular, are captivated by this influencer culture. They idolize these online personalities and strive to emulate their lifestyles, looks, and success. This admiration can be both positive and negative. On one hand, influencers can provide valuable content, such as fitness routines, healthy recipes, and motivational messages, which can inspire teenagers to lead a healthier and more fulfilling life. On the other hand, the constant exposure to curated and edited content can create unrealistic expectations and foster feelings of inadequacy.

Parents, too, are not immune to the influence of this culture. They may be concerned about the impact influencers have on their teenagers' self-esteem, mental health, and spending habits. It is crucial for parents to engage in open and honest conversations with their children about the limitations and realities of influencer culture. They should encourage their teenagers to think critically, question what they see online, and develop a healthy sense of self-worth that isn't solely based on external validation.

For aspiring influencers, this subchapter offers valuable insights into the world of social media and how to navigate it successfully. It delves into the importance of authenticity, creating genuine connections with followers, and maintaining a consistent brand. It also emphasizes the need for influencers to use their platform responsibly and ethically, considering the impact their content may have on impressionable minds.

In conclusion, the rise of influencer culture has transformed the way we consume media and interact with celebrities. It has its pros and cons, and it is essential for teenagers, parents, and even aspiring influencers themselves to be aware of the potential pitfalls and benefits. By understanding the influence influencers have and by promoting critical thinking and self-worth, we can navigate this new era of social media with confidence and grace.

The Importance of Building an Online Presence

In today's digital age, where the world is interconnected through social media platforms, building an online presence has become a crucial aspect of success, especially for teenagers, parents, and aspiring YouTubers. This subchapter will delve into the significance of establishing a strong online presence, particularly for individuals aspiring to become influencers or fitness and wellness influencers.

For teenagers, building an online presence can provide a platform to express their creativity, showcase their talents, and connect with like-minded individuals worldwide. Whether it's through creating captivating videos, sharing insightful blog posts, or showcasing their artwork, teenagers can use the power of social media to amplify their voices and gain recognition. Moreover, cultivating an online presence allows teenagers to build valuable skills such as digital marketing, content creation, and networking – skills that will undoubtedly benefit them in their future endeavors.

Parents, too, can benefit from building an online presence. By establishing an engaging social media presence, parents can connect with other parents, share their experiences, and gain support and advice. Additionally, parents can leverage their online presence to promote their businesses or advocate for causes they are passionate about. Building an online presence not only provides a platform for parents to share their knowledge and expertise but also enables them to connect with a broader audience and create meaningful relationships.

For aspiring YouTubers, an online presence is the key to success. Building a dedicated fan base and gaining subscribers is only possible when one establishes a strong online presence. By consistently creating high-quality content, engaging with viewers, and utilizing effective marketing strategies, YouTubers can build a loyal following and increase their chances of success.

An online presence also allows YouTubers to collaborate with other content creators, attract brand partnerships, and monetize their channels.

Furthermore, for fitness and wellness influencers, an online presence is essential to inspire and motivate others on their journey towards a healthier lifestyle. By sharing fitness tips, workout routines, and wellness advice, influencers can make a positive impact on their followers' lives. Building an online presence also allows fitness and wellness influencers to create communities, share success stories, and provide a platform for individuals to connect and support one another.

In conclusion, building an online presence has become a vital aspect of success in today's digital world. Whether you are a teenager, parent, or aspiring YouTuber in the influencer or fitness and wellness influencer niche, establishing an engaging online presence allows you to showcase your talents, connect with others, and make a positive impact. So, embrace the power of social media, harness your creativity, and build a strong online presence that sets you on the path to success.

The Basics of Becoming a Fitness and Wellness Influencer

Identifying Your Passion and Niche

The journey to becoming a successful influencer in the world of social media begins with one important question: What are you truly passionate about? For teenagers, parents, and aspiring YouTubers looking to make their mark, finding your passion and niche is the crucial first step towards mastering the social media game. In this subchapter, we will explore the importance of identifying your passion and niche, and how it can set you on the path to becoming a successful influencer, specifically in the realm of fitness and wellness.

Passion is the fuel that drives your content and connects you with your audience. It is what sets you apart from others and gives your content a unique flavor. Take the time to reflect on what truly excites you, whether it's fitness, wellness, or any other area of interest. Identifying your passion will not only make your content more authentic and enjoyable to create, but it will also attract like-minded individuals who resonate with your message.

Once you have identified your passion, it's time to narrow down your niche. A niche is a specific area within your passion that you can specialize in. For example, within the fitness and wellness industry, you could focus on yoga, weightlifting, healthy recipes, or mental health. By honing in on a specific niche, you become an expert in that field and build credibility among your audience.

To identify your niche, ask yourself what makes you unique. What knowledge or expertise can you bring to the table? Consider your personal experiences, skills, and interests. Don't be afraid to think outside the box and carve your own path. Remember, finding a niche doesn't mean limiting yourself; it means creating a space where your passion can flourish.

Furthermore, understanding your target audience is essential in determining your niche. As a teenager or parent, you may have insights into the struggles and aspirations of your peers or children. This knowledge can be invaluable in tailoring your content to meet the needs of your target audience. Aspiring YouTubers can analyze popular trends and identify gaps in the market to find their unique niche.

In conclusion, identifying your passion and niche is the foundation for success in the world of social media influence. By aligning your content with your true passions and specializing in a specific niche, you will create authentic, engaging content that resonates with your audience. Whether you aspire to become a fitness influencer, a wellness guru, or any other type of influencer, the key lies in finding what sets your soul on fire and sharing it with the world. So, take the time to explore your passions, define your niche, and let your influence soar.

Developing Your Personal Brand

In today's digital age, where social media has become an integral part of our lives, it is more important than ever to develop a strong personal brand. Whether you're a teenager trying to make your mark in the world, a parent looking to navigate the online space, or a budding YouTuber seeking to carve out your niche, understanding the art of developing your personal brand is crucial. This subchapter will guide you through the essential steps to create a unique and impactful brand that resonates with your target audience.

First and foremost, it is essential to identify your niche. As an influencer, fitness enthusiast, or wellness advocate, you need to determine your area of expertise and passion. What sets you apart from others in the industry? What value can you provide to your audience? By answering these questions, you can establish a clear direction for your personal brand.

Once you have defined your niche, it's time to craft your brand identity. This includes creating a compelling name, logo, and color scheme that align with your content and resonate with your target audience. Consistency is key here –

ensure that your branding elements are present across all your social media platforms to build recognition and familiarity.

Next, focus on content creation. As an influencer, your content is the backbone of your personal brand. Share valuable information, engaging stories, and inspiring content that reflects your expertise and resonates with your audience. Be authentic and genuine, as this will help you build trust and establish meaningful connections with your followers.

Furthermore, leverage the power of social media to amplify your brand. Identify the platforms where your target audience is most active and create a strong presence there. Engage with your followers, respond to comments and messages, and collaborate with other influencers to expand your reach. Remember, social media is not just a one-way communication channel – it's a community where you can connect, inspire, and be inspired.

Lastly, always be mindful of your online reputation. In the digital world, everything you post and share contributes to your personal brand. Be cautious about the content you share, ensure it aligns with your brand values, and maintain a positive and respectful online presence. Your reputation is your most valuable asset, so protect it wisely.

Developing your personal brand is an ongoing journey. Continuously analyze your audience's preferences and adapt your strategies accordingly. Embrace feedback, learn from your mistakes, and keep evolving. By mastering the art of developing your personal brand, you can position yourself as a reputable influencer, fitness guru, or wellness advocate, and make a lasting impact on your target audience.

Creating Engaging Content

In the world of social media, creating engaging content is the key to success. Whether you're a teenager, parent, or aspiring YouTuber in the influencer or fitness and wellness niche, understanding how to create content that captivates your audience is crucial. In this subchapter, we will explore effective strategies to help you create engaging content that leaves a lasting impact on your followers.

1. Know Your Audience: As an influencer, it's essential to understand who your target audience is. Teenagers, parents, and fitness and wellness enthusiasts have different needs and interests. By understanding your audience's preferences, you can tailor your content to meet their expectations. Conduct research, engage with your followers, and listen to their feedback to gain valuable insights.

2. Tell a Story: People love stories, and storytelling is a powerful tool to engage your audience. Whether you're sharing your personal fitness journey or giving parenting advice, weave your content into a compelling narrative. This will captivate your audience, making them more likely to connect with you on an emotional level.

3. Be Authentic: Authenticity is key in the world of social media. Teenagers, parents, and fitness and wellness enthusiasts want to connect with real people who share genuine experiences and opinions. Don't be afraid to show your vulnerabilities and be transparent about your struggles. Authenticity allows your audience to relate to you, creating a stronger bond.

4. Utilize Visuals: In a visually-driven world, captivating images and videos are essential. Use high-quality visuals that are aesthetically pleasing and aligned with your brand. Incorporate eye-catching thumbnails, engaging captions, and compelling video editing techniques to stand out from the crowd.

5. Encourage Interaction: Engaging content should encourage your audience to interact with you. Ask thought-provoking questions, create polls, and initiate discussions to promote active participation. Respond promptly to comments and messages, making your audience feel valued and heard.

6. Stay Consistent: Consistency is crucial to maintain your audience's interest. Set a content schedule and stick to it. Whether you're posting daily, weekly, or monthly, be consistent with your content delivery. This will build anticipation among your followers and keep them engaged.

7. Adapt and Innovate: Social media is constantly evolving, and it's important to adapt and innovate to stay relevant. Keep an eye on the latest trends and techniques in your niche. Experiment with new content formats, such as live streaming or IGTV, to keep your audience engaged and excited.

Remember, creating engaging content is a continuous learning process. Stay open to feedback, analyze your metrics, and adapt your strategies accordingly. By following these tips, you will be well on your way to mastering the art of creating engaging content and succeeding in the social media game.

Building Your Social Media Platform

Choosing the Right Social Media Channels

In today's digital age, social media has become an integral part of our lives. It allows us to connect with others, share our thoughts and experiences, and even build successful careers as influencers. However, with so many different social media platforms available, it can be overwhelming to decide which ones are the best fit for your goals and objectives. In this subchapter, we will explore the art of choosing the right social media channels to help teenagers, parents, and YouTubers navigate this vast online landscape.

For teenagers, social media can be a powerful tool for self-expression, staying connected with friends, and exploring their interests. However, it is crucial to choose platforms that prioritize privacy and safety. Popular choices among teenagers include Instagram, Snapchat, and TikTok. These platforms offer various features such as filters, stories, and short videos, allowing teenagers to showcase their creativity and connect with like-minded individuals.

Parents, on the other hand, may have different goals for using social media. They may seek to connect with other parents, share parenting tips, or stay updated on current events. Facebook groups and parenting forums are excellent options for parents as they provide a supportive community and valuable resources. Additionally, platforms like LinkedIn can be beneficial for parents looking to expand their professional network.

For YouTubers and aspiring influencers, an in-depth understanding of social media channels is essential. YouTube itself is an excellent platform for content creation, especially for those in the fitness and wellness niche. However, it's important to leverage other platforms to increase visibility and reach a broader audience. Instagram, for instance, allows influencers to share snippets of their content, engage with followers, and collaborate with brands. Twitter, on the other hand, is great for sharing quick updates and connecting with industry professionals.

When choosing the right social media channels, it is crucial to consider your target audience and niche. Fitness and wellness influencers may find platforms like Instagram, YouTube, and Pinterest particularly useful as they allow for visual content creation and provide opportunities for monetization through sponsorships and partnerships.

In conclusion, choosing the right social media channels is a crucial step towards mastering the social media game. Teenagers, parents, and YouTubers must carefully evaluate their goals, target audience, and niche before diving into the vast world of social media. By understanding the unique features and benefits of each platform, individuals can effectively communicate their message, build their brand, and connect with others in a meaningful way.

Optimizing Your Profile and Bio

In today's digital age, your online presence is more crucial than ever. Whether you're a teenager, parent, or aspiring YouTuber, understanding how to optimize your social media profiles and bios is essential to make a lasting impression and build a strong personal brand. This subchapter titled "Optimizing Your Profile and Bio" from the book "The Art of Influence: Mastering the Social Media Game" is specifically tailored to teenagers, parents, and YouTubers in the niches of influencer and fitness and wellness influencer, offering valuable insights and practical tips to help you stand out in the digital realm.

Your profile and bio act as your virtual business card, providing a snapshot of who you are and what you have to offer. As an influencer, it's crucial to create a profile that captures your unique personality and resonates with your target audience. For fitness and wellness influencers, emphasizing your expertise and passion for leading a healthy lifestyle is key. This subchapter will guide you through the process of optimizing your profile and bio to attract more followers and increase engagement.

Learn how to craft a compelling bio that effectively communicates your personal brand and captures the attention of potential followers. Discover the importance of using strategic keywords and hashtags to enhance your visibility and reach on social media platforms. Understand the significance of consistency in your profile layout, color scheme, and overall aesthetics to create a visually appealing and cohesive brand image.

Additionally, this subchapter will delve into the importance of regularly updating your profile and bio to reflect your growth and evolving interests, as well as the significance of engaging with your audience through comments, direct messages, and collaborations. It will also address the significance of maintaining a positive online presence, avoiding controversial or offensive content, and protecting your privacy.

By optimizing your profile and bio, you'll not only attract more followers but also establish yourself as a credible and influential figure in your niche. Whether you're a teenager looking to showcase your talents, a parent trying to navigate the social media world, or a YouTuber aspiring to build a loyal following, this subchapter will equip you with the knowledge and tools to optimize your online presence and master the social media game.

Creating Impactful Content

Growing Your Follower Base

Planning Your Content Strategy

In the ever-evolving world of social media, it has become increasingly important to have a well-thought-out content strategy. Whether you are a teenager looking to build your personal brand, a parent wanting to monitor your child's online presence, or a budding fitness and wellness influencer, understanding the power of planning your content is crucial. This subchapter will delve into the key elements and steps involved in creating an effective content strategy that will help you stand out in the crowded online space.

1. Define Your Goals: Before diving into creating content, it is essential to define your goals. Are you aiming to gain more followers, promote a healthy lifestyle, or simply express yourself creatively? Understanding your objectives will shape the direction of your content and help you stay focused on what truly matters to you.

2. Know Your Audience: Tailoring your content to your target audience is vital for capturing their attention and building a loyal following. As a teenager, your content may resonate more with your peers, while parents might focus on providing educational and informative content. Fitness and wellness influencers can craft content that inspires and motivates their audience to lead healthier lives. Understanding who you are speaking to will allow you to create content that truly resonates.

3. Content Types and Formats: Explore different content types and formats to keep your audience engaged. As a teenager, you can experiment with vlogs, challenges, or lifestyle content. Parents may choose to share parenting tips, family recipes, or stories about their experiences. Fitness and wellness influencers can showcase workout routines, healthy recipes, or provide informative videos related to their niche.

4. Consistency and Quality: Consistency is key to maintaining an active and engaged audience. Develop a content schedule that aligns with your goals and commit to it. However, do not sacrifice quality for quantity. It is better to produce fewer pieces of high-quality content that resonate with your audience than to flood your followers' feeds with subpar content.

5. Engagement and Interaction: Social media is all about building connections and engaging with your audience. Respond to comments, ask questions, and encourage discussions. This will help you build a community around your content and foster a sense of belonging.

By planning your content strategy, you can navigate the social media landscape with confidence. Whether you are a teenager, parent, or fitness and wellness influencer, understanding your goals, audience, content types, consistency, and engagement are essential for mastering the social media game. So take the time to strategize and watch your online presence flourish.

Crafting Compelling Captions and Visuals

In the digital age, where attention spans are shorter than ever, captivating your audience is crucial. Whether you're an aspiring influencer, a fitness enthusiast, or a wellness advocate, mastering the art of crafting compelling captions and visuals is essential for success in the social media game. This subchapter will provide you with valuable insights and tips to engage your audience effectively.

1. Know your audience: Understanding your target audience is the first step towards creating captivating content. For teenagers, parents, and YouTubers, it's important to tailor your captions and visuals to their interests, desires, and pain points. Research their preferences and trends to craft content that resonates with them.

2. Storytelling through captions: Captions are more than just a description of your visuals; they are an opportunity to tell a story. Use compelling narratives,

personal anecdotes, or thought-provoking questions to capture your audience's attention. Be authentic, relatable, and inject your unique personality into your captions.

3. Visuals that stand out: In a sea of content, your visuals need to be eye-catching and memorable. Whether it's through high-quality photos, engaging videos, or creative graphics, invest time and effort in creating visually appealing content. Experiment with different styles, filters, and compositions to find what resonates best with your audience.

4. Consistency is key: Building a strong online presence requires consistency in both your captions and visuals. Develop a consistent tone of voice that aligns with your brand and stick to it. Create a visual identity by using consistent colors, fonts, and layouts. This will help your audience recognize and connect with your content instantly.

5. Call-to-action: Encourage your audience to engage with your content by including a call-to-action in your captions. Whether it's asking them to comment, share, or tag a friend, make it clear what you want them to do. This helps in building a loyal and interactive community around your content.

Remember, crafting compelling captions and visuals is an ongoing process. Continuously analyze your engagement metrics, listen to feedback, and adapt your content accordingly. By understanding your audience, telling stories, creating standout visuals, and being consistent, you'll be well on your way to mastering the social media game and becoming a successful influencer or fitness and wellness advocate.

Incorporating Video and Storytelling

In today's digital age, social media has become a powerful tool for communication and self-expression. With platforms like YouTube, Instagram, and TikTok, anyone can become an influencer and make a significant impact on their audience. However, standing out from the crowd and building a loyal following requires more than just posting random videos or pictures. It demands the art of storytelling and incorporating videos to create compelling content that resonates with your viewers.

For teenagers, parents, and aspiring YouTubers, understanding the importance of incorporating video and storytelling can be the key to success in the social media game. Video has the ability to capture attention and convey emotions like no other medium. By combining it with storytelling techniques, you can create content that not only entertains but also inspires and influences your audience.

As an influencer, you have the power to shape the thoughts and behaviors of your followers. Whether you are an influencer in the fitness or wellness niche, your content should not only showcase your expertise but also tell a story that connects with your viewers on a personal level. By sharing your own struggles, triumphs, and journey towards a healthier lifestyle, you can inspire others to take charge of their well-being.

Parents and teenagers can also benefit from incorporating video and storytelling into their social media presence. By sharing their experiences and challenges as a family, parents can connect with other parents who may be facing similar situations. Teenagers, on the other hand, can use video and storytelling to express their thoughts, passions, and concerns, creating a sense of community and understanding among their peers.

Incorporating video and storytelling is not just about creating content that looks good; it's about creating content that makes an impact. Whether you are a teenager, a parent, or an aspiring YouTuber, understanding the art of storytelling and using videos as a medium can help you connect with your audience on a deeper level.

So, whether you are documenting your fitness journey, sharing wellness tips, or showcasing your daily life as a family, remember to incorporate video and storytelling into your content strategy. By doing so, you can captivate your audience and inspire them to take action, making a lasting impact in the social media world.

Engaging with Your Audience

Understanding Your Target Audience

As an influencer or aspiring influencer in the digital realm, it is crucial to understand your target audience. Whether you are a teenager, a parent, or a YouTuber, comprehending who your audience is and what they desire is vital for success in the social media game. This subchapter will explore the importance of understanding your target audience and provide you with valuable insights on how to connect with them effectively.

For teenagers, the online world is their playground, and they spend a significant portion of their time on social media platforms. Understanding this unique demographic is crucial for any influencer targeting them. Teenagers are seeking relatable content that mirrors their interests, challenges, and aspirations. By understanding their preferences, concerns, and trends, you can create content that resonates with them, fostering a strong connection and engagement.

Parents, on the other hand, have a different set of concerns and interests. As an influencer targeting parents, it is essential to recognize their values, priorities, and challenges. Parents often seek advice, inspiration, and guidance in various areas, from parenting tips to maintaining a healthy work-life balance. By providing valuable content that addresses their needs and concerns, you can establish yourself as a trusted resource and build a loyal following.

For YouTubers, understanding your target audience is crucial for maintaining and growing your subscriber base. Each YouTube channel caters to a specific niche, such as fitness and wellness. In this niche, your target audience consists of individuals passionate about leading a healthy lifestyle, seeking fitness tips, workout routines, and wellness advice. By understanding their desires and struggles, you can deliver content that adds value to their lives and keeps them coming back for more.

Moreover, as a fitness and wellness influencer, knowing your target audience's preferences, aspirations, and pain points will enable you to tailor your content effectively. Whether it is sharing workout routines, providing nutritional guidance, or discussing mental well-being, understanding your audience will help you create content that resonates with them and inspires positive change.

In conclusion, understanding your target audience is a fundamental aspect of mastering the social media game. Whether you are a teenager, a parent, or a YouTuber in the fitness and wellness niche, comprehending your audience's desires, interests, and challenges will allow you to create content that truly connects with them. By building a strong bond with your audience, you can enhance your influence and achieve success in the ever-evolving world of social media.

Building a Community

In an age where social media has become an integral part of our lives, building a community has never been more important. Whether you are a teenager, a parent, or a YouTuber, understanding the art of building a community can be a game-changer. This subchapter will guide you through the steps to create a strong and engaged community, specifically tailored to the niches of influencers and fitness and wellness influencers.

As a teenager, the desire to connect with like-minded individuals is natural. Building a community allows you to find your tribe, a group of people who share similar interests, passions, and goals. Social media platforms like Instagram and TikTok have become hotspots for teenagers to connect, share ideas, and support one another. By engaging with others, participating in discussions, and showcasing your unique personality, you can establish a strong presence within your community. Remember, it's not about the number of followers you have, but rather the quality of connections you make.

For parents, building a community can provide a support system and a platform to exchange experiences and advice. Parenting can be challenging, but knowing that you are not alone can make a significant difference. Joining online groups, attending virtual workshops, and engaging with other parents through social media can help you find solace, gain valuable insights, and build lasting relationships. By actively participating in discussions, sharing your own experiences, and offering support to others, you can contribute to a thriving community of parents.

As a YouTuber, building a community is essential for sustained success. Your subscribers are more than just numbers; they are a loyal community that supports and engages with your content. Interacting with your audience through comments, live streams, and social media platforms can foster a sense of belonging and connection. Additionally, collaboration with other YouTubers and influencers within your niche can help expand your reach and introduce you to new audiences. Remember to always provide value to your community, listen to their feedback, and create content that resonates with their interests and needs.

For fitness and wellness influencers, building a community is crucial to inspire and motivate others on their health journey. Sharing your own experiences, offering practical tips, and providing a safe space for discussion can help your followers stay committed to their fitness goals. Encouraging them to share their progress, asking for their input, and recognizing their achievements can foster a sense of belonging within your community. By creating a supportive and uplifting environment, you can empower others to prioritize their health and well-being.

In conclusion, building a community is an integral aspect of mastering the social media game. Whether you are a teenager, a parent, or a YouTuber in the niches of influencers or fitness and wellness, understanding the importance of community building can unlock a world of opportunities. By actively engaging with others, providing value, and creating a supportive environment, you can cultivate a thriving community that will support and uplift you on your journey. Remember, it's not about the numbers, but the meaningful connections you make along the way.

Responding to Comments and Messages

In today's digital age, where social media has become an integral part of our lives, it is crucial to understand the importance of responding to comments and messages. Whether you are a teenager, parent, or a budding YouTuber, knowing how to effectively engage with your audience is key to mastering the social media game. This subchapter will guide you through the art of responding to comments and messages, ensuring that you build strong relationships with your followers and maintain a positive online presence.

For teenagers, social media platforms offer a space to express themselves and connect with like-minded individuals. However, it is essential to remember that your online presence is a reflection of your character. When responding to comments and messages, always maintain a respectful tone. Address any concerns or questions your followers may have, and encourage open dialogue. Remember, your words hold influence, and by responding thoughtfully, you can foster a supportive and inclusive community.

Parents, as your children navigate the world of social media, it is crucial to guide them in their online interactions. Teach them the importance of responding to comments and messages promptly, as it showcases their commitment to their audience. Additionally, encourage them to engage in meaningful conversations, but also educate them about the potential dangers of sharing personal information. By instilling these values, you empower your children to become responsible digital citizens.

For aspiring YouTubers, responding to comments and messages is a vital aspect of growing your channel. Take the time to acknowledge your viewers, as they are the backbone of your success. Responding to their comments not only shows appreciation but also encourages them to continue engaging with your content. Remember, building a loyal audience requires consistent interaction and genuine connections.

In the niche of fitness and wellness influencers, responding to comments and messages is an opportunity to provide valuable guidance and support to your followers. Whether they seek advice on workouts, nutrition, or mental health, take the time to address their concerns individually. By doing so, you establish credibility and trust within your community, ultimately expanding your influence.

In conclusion, responding to comments and messages is an integral part of mastering the social media game. Whether you are a teenager, parent, or a budding YouTuber in the influencer or fitness and wellness niche, understanding the art of engagement is crucial. By responding thoughtfully, respectfully, and promptly, you can build strong relationships with your audience, foster a positive online presence, and ultimately thrive in the world of social media.

Collaborations and Partnerships

Leveraging Influencer Collaborations

In this digital age, social media has become an integral part of our lives. It has revolutionized the way we connect, communicate, and consume content. One of the most powerful aspects of social media is the rise of influencers. These individuals have built a loyal following and have the ability to influence the opinions and behaviors of their audience. This subchapter will delve into the world of leveraging influencer collaborations, specifically targeting teenagers, parents, and YouTubers, with a focus on the influencer, fitness, and wellness niches.

For teenagers, influencers play a significant role in shaping their interests, trends, and aspirations. By collaborating with influencers, teenagers can gain valuable insights and guidance. Whether it's fashion, beauty, or lifestyle, influencers can provide a fresh perspective and offer advice on various aspects of their lives. They can also serve as role models, inspiring teenagers to pursue their passions and make informed decisions.

Parents, on the other hand, can benefit from influencer collaborations by gaining access to expert knowledge and resources. Influencers in the parenting niche can offer valuable tips, tricks, and insights on raising children, managing household responsibilities, and maintaining a balanced lifestyle. By leveraging influencer collaborations, parents can enhance their parenting skills, discover new products and services, and connect with a supportive community.

For YouTubers, collaborating with influencers can be a game-changer. By partnering with influencers, YouTubers can tap into new audiences, expand their reach, and gain credibility. Influencers bring their unique perspectives and expertise, adding value to the content and creating a win-win situation for both parties. Whether it's a joint video, a sponsored post, or a cross-promotion, influencer collaborations can significantly boost a YouTuber's growth and success.

In the fitness and wellness industry, influencers have become instrumental in promoting healthy living and inspiring others to adopt an active lifestyle. By collaborating with fitness and wellness influencers, individuals can gain access to workout routines, nutritional advice, and motivational content. These collaborations can provide valuable guidance and support to those looking to improve their physical and mental well-being.

In conclusion, leveraging influencer collaborations can be a powerful tool for teenagers, parents, and YouTubers within the influencer, fitness, and wellness niches. By tapping into the expertise, knowledge, and influence of these individuals, audiences can gain valuable insights, inspiration, and support. Whether you're a teenager seeking guidance, a parent looking for parenting advice, or a YouTuber aiming to expand your reach, influencer collaborations can help you master the social media game and achieve your goals.

Building Relationships with Brands

One of the most exciting aspects of being an influencer, whether you're a teenager, parent, or a YouTuber in the fitness and wellness niche, is the opportunity to collaborate with brands. Not only does this provide you with a chance to showcase your talent and expertise, but it also opens up doors for potential sponsorships and partnerships that can significantly boost your online presence. This subchapter aims to guide you through the process of building strong and lasting relationships with brands, ensuring mutual benefits and growth.

First and foremost, it's crucial to establish your personal brand and niche before reaching out to any brands. Define your unique selling proposition and understand your target audience. This clarity will not only attract the right brands but also empower you to create content that resonates with your followers.

Next, start researching brands that align with your values and content. Look for companies that share your passion for fitness, wellness, and healthy living.

Check their social media presence, website, and previous collaborations to ensure they have a genuine interest in working with influencers.

Once you've identified a brand you'd like to collaborate with, start engaging with their content. Like, comment, and share their posts to demonstrate your interest and support. Brands appreciate influencers who genuinely interact with their content and show enthusiasm for their products or services.

When you feel ready to reach out, craft a professional and personalized pitch. Introduce yourself, explain why you're interested in collaborating with the brand, and highlight how your audience aligns with their target market. Share any relevant metrics, such as your engagement rate or follower demographics, to demonstrate the value you can bring to the partnership.

Remember that building relationships takes time and effort. Be patient and consistent in your interactions with brands. Even if they don't respond immediately, continue engaging with their content and showcase your dedication to their brand.

Finally, once you've secured a collaboration, deliver exceptional content that aligns with both your personal brand and the brand you're working with. Be creative, authentic, and transparent with your audience about the partnership. Building trust with your followers is essential for maintaining long-term relationships with brands.

In conclusion, building relationships with brands as an influencer in the fitness and wellness niche offers immense opportunities for growth and success. By establishing your personal brand, researching compatible brands, engaging with their content, and delivering exceptional content, you can create mutually beneficial partnerships that propel your influence and impact to new heights.

Negotiating Sponsorships and Brand Deals

In the fast-paced world of social media and influencer marketing, negotiating sponsorships and brand deals is a crucial skill for teenagers, parents, and YouTubers alike. Whether you are an aspiring influencer or a fitness and wellness enthusiast looking to monetize your passion, understanding the art of negotiation can significantly impact your success in the industry.

This subchapter delves into the strategies and techniques necessary for securing lucrative sponsorships and brand deals in the realm of social media. From building your personal brand to approaching potential sponsors, here's a comprehensive guide to help you master the art of negotiation.

1. Building Your Personal Brand: Before diving into negotiations, it's essential to establish a strong personal brand. Define your niche as an influencer or fitness and wellness enthusiast and create engaging content that resonates with your target audience. A well-defined personal brand will attract sponsors and increase your bargaining power.

2. Identifying Potential Sponsors: Research and identify brands that align with your personal brand and audience. Look for companies that share similar values and offer products or services that your followers would genuinely benefit from. This alignment will make a compelling case for potential sponsors to collaborate with you.

3. Crafting a Winning Pitch: When approaching sponsors, create a well-crafted pitch that clearly communicates your value proposition. Highlight your audience demographics, engagement rates, and past successful collaborations. Showcase how your partnership can benefit both parties and drive meaningful results.

4. Negotiation Techniques: Negotiating sponsorships and brand deals requires finesse. Understand your worth and set realistic expectations. Consider factors

such as deliverables, exclusivity, duration, and compensation. Be prepared to negotiate and find a win-win agreement that satisfies both parties.

5. Long-Term Partnerships: Building long-term relationships with sponsors is beneficial for both parties. Focus on nurturing these relationships by consistently delivering high-quality content, exceeding expectations, and providing valuable insights to your sponsors. Long-term partnerships often lead to better deals and increased brand loyalty.

6. Legal Considerations: As you navigate the world of sponsorships and brand deals, it's crucial to understand the legal aspects. Familiarize yourself with influencer marketing guidelines, disclose sponsored content transparently, and consider seeking professional advice to ensure compliance with regulations.

Negotiating sponsorships and brand deals is a continuous learning process. By mastering the art of negotiation and building strong relationships with sponsors, you can turn your passion into a profitable venture. Keep refining your skills, stay authentic, and never stop striving for success in the dynamic world of social media influence.

Monetizing Your Influence

Exploring Different Revenue Streams

In the world of social media, where influence is everything, it's important to not only build a strong online presence but also explore various revenue streams. As a teenager, parent, or aspiring YouTuber in the influencer or fitness and wellness niche, understanding and diversifying your income sources can make all the difference in your online success.

One of the most common ways influencers generate revenue is through brand collaborations and sponsorships. As your follower count grows, brands will start to take notice of your influence and may approach you for partnerships. These collaborations can range from sponsored posts, product reviews, or even ambassadorship programs. Remember to only collaborate with brands that align with your values and interests, as authenticity is key to maintaining your audience's trust.

Another revenue stream to explore is affiliate marketing. This involves promoting products or services through unique links provided by companies. When your followers make a purchase using your link, you earn a percentage of the sale as a commission. This can be a great way to monetize your content without relying solely on sponsored collaborations.

Additionally, consider creating and selling your own merchandise. Your loyal followers are often eager to support you by purchasing items that represent your personal brand. Whether it's clothing, accessories, or even digital products like e-books or online courses, creating merchandise can be a lucrative revenue stream while also strengthening your connection with your audience.

For those in the fitness and wellness niche, offering personalized coaching or training programs can be a valuable source of income. Many people are willing to invest in expert guidance to help them reach their health and fitness goals. Whether you choose to offer one-on-one coaching, group programs, or even digital workout plans, providing value and expertise can attract paying clients.

Lastly, don't underestimate the power of YouTube's monetization program. As your channel grows, you may become eligible for YouTube's Partner Program, allowing you to earn revenue through ads displayed on your videos. However, keep in mind that building a substantial subscriber base and consistently creating high-quality content is crucial for this revenue stream to be significant.

In conclusion, exploring different revenue streams is essential for success in the social media game. As a teenager, parent, or aspiring YouTuber in the influencer or fitness and wellness niche, consider brand collaborations, affiliate marketing, merchandise creation, personalized coaching, and YouTube monetization as potential sources of income. Remember, building a strong online presence and maintaining authenticity are key to attracting brands and building a loyal audience willing to support your journey.

Creating and Selling Merchandise

In the fast-paced world of social media, influencers have become household names. From makeup tutorials to fitness challenges, these individuals have managed to capture the attention of millions of followers. But what sets apart successful influencers from the rest? It's their ability to monetize their brand through merchandise.

For teenagers aspiring to become influencers, creating and selling merchandise can be a game-changer. Not only does it give you an opportunity to connect with your fans on a deeper level, but it also allows you to establish yourself as a serious player in the industry. So how can you go about creating and selling merchandise effectively?

First and foremost, it's essential to have a clear understanding of your brand. Define your niche as an influencer – whether it's fitness, wellness, or any other area of expertise. This will help you identify the type of merchandise that will resonate with your audience. For example, if you're a fitness influencer, your fans might be interested in workout gear, water bottles, or even fitness journals.

Once you have a clear vision, it's time to design your merchandise. Consider collaborating with a graphic designer to create unique and eye-catching designs that reflect your personal brand. Remember, the key is to create products that your followers will be proud to wear or use. Quality matters, so ensure that the materials used are durable and long-lasting.

Next, you need to set up an online store. Platforms like Shopify or Etsy make it easy to create an e-commerce website without any technical knowledge. Make sure your store is visually appealing and user-friendly. Provide detailed product descriptions and high-quality images to entice potential buyers.

Promotion is crucial when it comes to selling merchandise. Leverage your social media platforms to create buzz around your products. Post high-quality images wearing or using your merchandise and encourage your followers to do the same. Consider running giveaways or collaborations with other influencers to boost visibility. Don't forget to engage with your audience, answer their questions, and address any concerns they may have.

Lastly, shipping and customer service are vital for a successful merchandise business. Ensure that your shipping process is efficient and reliable. Offer various shipping options to cater to different customer needs. Additionally, make it a priority to provide excellent customer service. Respond to inquiries promptly and handle any returns or exchanges professionally.

Creating and selling merchandise is an excellent way for influencers to monetize their brand and engage with their audience. By following these tips, teenagers, parents, and fitness and wellness influencers can take their social media game to the next level. Remember, success doesn't happen overnight, but with dedication and creativity, your merchandise business can thrive.

Maximizing Affiliate Marketing

In the fast-paced world of social media, affiliate marketing has emerged as a powerful tool for influencers and content creators to monetize their platforms. Whether you're a teenager looking to make some extra income, a parent seeking financial stability, or a fitness and wellness influencer aiming to expand your reach, mastering the art of affiliate marketing can be a game-changer.

Affiliate marketing essentially involves promoting products or services on your social media platforms and earning a commission for every sale made through your unique affiliate link. It's a win-win situation where you get to monetize your influence, while your audience benefits from discovering new and valuable products.

For teenagers eager to dip their toes into the world of affiliate marketing, it's crucial to focus on authenticity and credibility. Honesty is key; only promote products you genuinely believe in and that align with your personal brand. Building trust with your audience is vital for long-term success. Additionally, leverage your social media platforms to showcase your unique personality and engage with your followers. By creating a genuine connection, you'll increase the likelihood of them purchasing products through your affiliate links.

Parents can also tap into the vast potential of affiliate marketing to supplement their income or even turn it into a full-time career. As a parent, authenticity is equally important. However, you can also leverage your parenting experience to connect with brands catering to families and children. Promote products that you have personally tried and tested with your own family, and share your honest opinions. Your relatability will resonate with other parents, leading to higher engagement and conversions.

For fitness and wellness influencers, affiliate marketing offers a plethora of opportunities to collaborate with brands in the health and wellness industry. Share your fitness journey, tips, and advice with your audience, and recommend products that have helped you achieve your goals. This way, you not only inspire your followers but also provide them with valuable recommendations that can enhance their own fitness journeys.

To maximize your success in affiliate marketing, it's crucial to consistently track your performance, experiment with different strategies, and optimize your content based on the results. Keep an eye on your click-through rates and conversion rates to identify what works best for your audience. Additionally, stay up to date with the latest trends and innovations in the industry to stay ahead of the competition.

In conclusion, affiliate marketing is a powerful tool for teenagers, parents, and fitness and wellness influencers to monetize their social media platforms. By focusing on authenticity, credibility, and building genuine connections with your audience, you can maximize your success in the ever-evolving world of affiliate marketing.

Staying Authentic and Ethical

Maintaining Transparency with Your Audience

In today's digital age, where social media rules the world, maintaining transparency with your audience is paramount, whether you are a teenager, parent, or a YouTuber. In this subchapter, we will delve into the importance of being open, honest, and authentic in the online world, particularly for influencers and fitness and wellness influencers.

For teenagers, social media platforms have become an integral part of their lives. However, it is crucial for them to understand the significance of transparency. Being transparent means being genuine and real, not just presenting a filtered version of oneself. By staying true to who they are, teenagers can build a loyal following and inspire others. It's essential for them to remember that their audience is looking for authenticity, not a facade.

As parents, it is crucial to guide your children in maintaining transparency on social media. Encourage them to be open about their experiences, both positive and negative. Teach them the value of sharing their struggles and how they overcame them. By doing so, they can not only inspire others but also create a safe space where their peers can open up and seek support.

For YouTubers and influencers, transparency is the key to building trust with their audience. While it may be tempting to portray a perfect life, being honest about the ups and downs of their journey is what truly connects them with their followers. Sharing personal stories, discussing challenges they faced, and even admitting mistakes can make them relatable and approachable. The audience appreciates influencers who are not afraid to show their vulnerable side.

Fitness and wellness influencers, in particular, have a responsibility to maintain transparency. With health and fitness being such important aspects of people's lives, it is crucial for influencers in this niche to provide accurate and reliable information. Sharing their own fitness journey, discussing the science behind various workouts or diets, and debunking myths can help their audience make informed decisions about their own well-being.

In conclusion, maintaining transparency with your audience is essential in the world of social media. Whether you are a teenager, parent, or a YouTuber, being open, honest, and authentic will not only help you build trust but also inspire others. By sharing your experiences, struggles, and successes, you create a genuine connection with your audience. So embrace transparency and let it be the foundation of your online presence.

Balancing Personal and Sponsored Content

In the fast-paced world of social media, where influencers dominate platforms like YouTube, Instagram, and TikTok, it is crucial to strike a balance between personal and sponsored content. As a teenager, parent, or aspiring influencer in the fitness and wellness niche, finding this equilibrium can be the key to building an authentic and successful online presence.

For teenagers exploring the world of social media, it is essential to understand the distinction between personal and sponsored content. Personal content is what truly reflects your personality, interests, and values. It allows you to connect with your audience on a deeper level, building a loyal following who genuinely relate to you. Sharing your personal experiences, struggles, and triumphs can inspire and motivate others, creating a real sense of community. However, it is important to maintain a level of privacy and not overshare personal details that could compromise your safety.

Sponsored content, on the other hand, involves partnerships with brands or companies who pay you to promote their products or services. While this can be a great way to monetize your platform and gain exposure, it's crucial to be selective about the brands you endorse. Ensure that their values align with your own and that the products are genuinely beneficial to your audience.

Transparency is vital when sharing sponsored content, so always disclose when a post is an advertisement.

Parents play a crucial role in guiding their teenagers through the world of social media. Encourage open communication and help them understand the importance of maintaining an authentic online presence. Teach them to value personal content and the impact it can have on others. Help them navigate the world of sponsored content, ensuring they are discerning about the brands they choose to promote.

For aspiring fitness and wellness influencers, striking a balance between personal and sponsored content is equally crucial. Your audience looks to you for inspiration, guidance, and expertise. Sharing your personal fitness journey, workout routines, and healthy recipes can be incredibly inspiring for your followers. However, sponsored content can provide opportunities for collaboration with fitness brands, showcasing their products and sharing valuable insights.

In conclusion, balancing personal and sponsored content is a skill that all teenagers, parents, and aspiring fitness and wellness influencers should cultivate. By maintaining authenticity, being selective with brand partnerships, and valuing personal content, you can build a successful online presence while positively impacting your audience. Remember, social media is a powerful tool, and using it responsibly and ethically is paramount.

Navigating Sponsored Content Guidelines

In today's digital world, social media has become a powerful tool for influencers and content creators to connect with their audience. However, with the rise of sponsored content, it is essential for teenagers, parents, and YouTubers to understand and navigate the guidelines surrounding these collaborations. In this subchapter, we will delve into the intricacies of sponsored content and how to maintain authenticity while abiding by the rules.

For teenagers who aspire to be influencers, it is crucial to understand that sponsored content comes with responsibilities. Firstly, always disclose when a post or video is sponsored. Transparency builds trust with your audience and ensures that they know you are promoting a product or service because you genuinely believe in it, not just for monetary gain.

Parents play a vital role in guiding their teenagers through the world of sponsored content. Encourage them to choose brands that align with their values and are relevant to their niche. It's important to educate them about the potential risks of promoting products that may not be safe or suitable for their target audience. By helping them make informed decisions, parents can safeguard their child's reputation and maintain a positive relationship with their followers.

YouTubers, especially fitness and wellness influencers, face unique challenges when it comes to sponsored content. Health-related products and services must be thoroughly researched to ensure they are safe and effective. As an influencer in this niche, you have a responsibility to promote fitness and wellness in a responsible and accurate manner. Be cautious of misleading claims and always back your recommendations with credible sources.

To navigate sponsored content guidelines successfully, it's crucial to stay up to date with the regulations set by the platform you are using. For example, YouTube has specific guidelines regarding disclosure, including the use of hashtags like #sponsored or #ad in the title or description of the video. Failure to comply with these rules could result in penalties and damage to your reputation.

In conclusion, sponsored content is an integral part of the influencer world, but it must be approached with care. Teenagers, parents, and YouTubers must understand and comply with the guidelines surrounding sponsored content to maintain authenticity and trust with their audience. By making informed decisions, staying transparent, and adhering to platform regulations, influencers can navigate this landscape successfully while making a positive impact on their followers' lives.

Overcoming Challenges and Staying Motivated

Dealing with Online Trolls and Hate

In today's digital age, where anyone can express their opinions and thoughts freely, it is no surprise that online trolls and hate have become a prevalent issue. Whether you are a teenager, parent, or a YouTuber in the influencer or fitness and wellness niches, dealing with online trolls and hate is something you may encounter on a regular basis. However, it is essential to understand that you have the power to control your online experience and protect your mental well-being.

First and foremost, it is important to remember that trolls and haters often seek attention and thrive on negative reactions. Responding to their hateful comments may only fuel their fire. Instead, try to maintain your composure and ignore their negativity. Surround yourself with positive people who support and uplift you, both online and offline. Seeking validation from strangers on the internet is a dangerous trap that can lead to a constant need for approval.

Another effective approach to dealing with online trolls and hate is to use moderation tools available on various social media platforms. These tools allow you to filter out offensive comments, block or mute certain users, and report abusive behavior. By utilizing these features, you can create a safer and more positive online environment for yourself and your followers.

Additionally, it is crucial to remember that you are not alone in this battle. Reach out to trusted friends, family members, or even professional counselors who can offer guidance and support. Talking about your experiences with someone who understands can provide you with a fresh perspective and help you regain your confidence.

For parents, it is essential to have open and honest conversations with your teenagers about online trolls and hate. Educate them about the importance of not taking hateful comments personally and the significance of prioritizing their mental well-being. Encourage them to use the available tools to protect themselves and remind them that their worth is not determined by the opinions of strangers on the internet.

Ultimately, dealing with online trolls and hate requires resilience, self-confidence, and a strong support system. By focusing on the positive aspects of your online presence and surrounding yourself with individuals who uplift you, you can navigate the social media landscape with grace and control. Remember, you have the power to influence your online experience and build a community that promotes kindness and respect.

Managing Burnout and Mental Health

In today's fast-paced world, managing burnout and maintaining good mental health has become increasingly important, especially for teenagers, parents, and YouTubers. This subchapter explores practical strategies for individuals in the influencer and fitness and wellness influencer niches to effectively manage burnout and prioritize mental well-being.

Burnout, a state of emotional, physical, and mental exhaustion caused by excessive and prolonged stress, can have detrimental effects on one's overall well-being and success. As an influencer or aspiring influencer, it's easy to get caught up in the pressure to constantly produce content, engage with followers, and maintain an active presence on social media platforms. However, neglecting your mental health can lead to burnout and negatively impact your ability to connect with your audience.

First and foremost, it is crucial to set boundaries and establish a healthy work-life balance. As a teenager or parent, it's important to allocate specific times for work and relaxation, ensuring that you have dedicated personal time to unwind and recharge. For YouTubers and influencers, it's essential to establish a schedule that allows for breaks, self-care activities, and time away from screens.

In addition, incorporating stress management techniques into your daily routine can help prevent burnout. This may include practicing mindfulness, meditation, or engaging in physical activities such as yoga or exercise. Prioritizing self-care activities, such as spending quality time with loved ones, pursuing hobbies, or engaging in creative outlets, can also contribute to maintaining good mental health.

Furthermore, reaching out for support is crucial in managing burnout and mental health. As a teenager, it's important to communicate with parents, friends, or trusted adults about any stressors or challenges you may be facing. For parents and YouTubers, seeking support from fellow influencers, joining online communities, or even considering therapy can provide valuable insights, advice, and a safe space to share experiences.

Remember, managing burnout and prioritizing mental health is not a sign of weakness but a testament to your strength and dedication to your well-being. By implementing these strategies and acknowledging the importance of self-care, you can navigate the challenges of being an influencer or fitness and wellness influencer while maintaining a healthy mind and body.

Seeking Support from Peers and Mentors

In the fast-paced world of social media and online influence, seeking support from peers and mentors is crucial for teenagers, parents, and aspiring YouTubers looking to make their mark in the industry. The journey to becoming a successful influencer, especially in the fitness and wellness niche, can be challenging and at times overwhelming. This subchapter aims to shed light on the importance of seeking support from those who have walked this path before, offering guidance, motivation, and valuable insights.

For teenagers venturing into the world of influence, seeking advice and support from peers who share similar aspirations can be immensely beneficial. Building a network of like-minded individuals can provide a sense of camaraderie and help overcome obstacles that often arise along the way. Engaging in online communities, forums, or attending influencer events can create opportunities for collaboration, brainstorming, and learning from the experiences of others.

Parents, on the other hand, play a crucial role in supporting and guiding their teenage children through their influencer journey. By actively participating in their child's social media endeavors, parents can not only ensure their safety but also offer valuable advice and provide a much-needed perspective on managing time, balancing responsibilities, and maintaining a healthy work-life balance.

For aspiring YouTubers in the fitness and wellness niche, seeking guidance from mentors who have already established themselves can be a game-changer. Mentors can offer practical advice on content creation, branding, and monetization strategies. Additionally, they can share their experiences, including the challenges they faced and the lessons they learned, helping new influencers avoid common pitfalls.

Mentorship programs, online courses, and even personal connections can connect aspiring influencers with experienced mentors. Engaging in mentor-mentee relationships can provide a unique opportunity for personal growth, skill development, and networking.

Remember, seeking support from peers and mentors is not a sign of weakness, but rather a proactive step towards success. By surrounding yourself with individuals who share your passion for influencing and have already achieved success, you can gain the confidence, knowledge, and inspiration needed to excel in the competitive world of social media.

In conclusion, seeking support from peers and mentors is a fundamental aspect of mastering the social media game. Whether you are a teenager, parent, or aspiring YouTuber in the fitness and wellness niche, building a network of like-minded individuals and seeking guidance from experienced mentors is key to overcoming challenges, gaining valuable insights, and ultimately reaching your full potential as an influencer. Embrace the power of support, and let it propel you towards your goals.

The Future of Social Media Influence

Embracing Emerging Platforms and Trends

In today's digital era, staying ahead of the game means embracing emerging platforms and trends. This subchapter explores how teenagers, parents, and YouTubers can navigate the ever-evolving world of social media to become successful influencers, especially in the niches of fitness and wellness.

For teenagers, social media platforms have become an integral part of their lives. It offers them a chance to express themselves, connect with like-minded individuals, and even build a personal brand. However, with new platforms constantly emerging, it can be overwhelming to know which ones are worth investing time and effort into. The key is to be open-minded and willing to explore new avenues. By keeping an eye on the pulse of emerging platforms, teenagers can position themselves as early adopters and gain a competitive edge in the influencer industry.

Parents, on the other hand, play a crucial role in guiding their teenagers through the social media landscape. They must stay informed about the platforms their children are using and understand the potential risks and benefits associated with each one. By embracing emerging platforms, parents can foster open lines of communication with their children and create a safe environment for them to explore their passions and interests.

For YouTubers, embracing emerging platforms and trends is essential to staying relevant and expanding their audience. YouTube itself has undergone numerous changes since its inception, and diversifying one's presence across platforms like Instagram, TikTok, or Snapchat can help reach a wider audience. By staying ahead of emerging trends, YouTubers can adapt their content to meet the changing demands of their viewers, ensuring they remain at the forefront of the influencer game.

In the niche of fitness and wellness, embracing emerging platforms and trends is particularly important. With the rise of fitness influencers, it is crucial to stay innovative and find new ways to engage with audiences. Platforms like Instagram and TikTok offer unique opportunities to showcase workouts, share healthy recipes, and inspire others to lead a healthy lifestyle. By embracing these emerging platforms, fitness and wellness influencers can establish themselves as authorities in their field and attract a dedicated following.

In conclusion, embracing emerging platforms and trends is vital for teenagers, parents, and YouTubers in the influencer industry, especially within the fitness and wellness niche. By staying adaptable, open-minded, and informed, individuals can leverage the power of social media to build their personal brand and influence others positively.

Adapting to Changes in Algorithms

In today's digital age, where social media platforms reign supreme, algorithms play a pivotal role in determining the visibility and success of content creators. Whether you're a teenager seeking to build a personal brand, a parent interested in understanding the social media landscape, or a fitness and wellness influencer navigating the online world, it is crucial to adapt to changes in algorithms. This subchapter will explore the significance of algorithmic changes and provide valuable insights on how to stay ahead of the game.

Algorithms are complex mathematical formulas used by social media platforms to deliver content to users based on their interests, engagement, and various other factors. These algorithms are constantly evolving, making it essential for influencers to stay updated and adapt their strategies accordingly. For teenagers aiming to become influencers, understanding algorithms is crucial to building a strong online presence. By keeping up with algorithmic changes, aspiring influencers can tailor their content to reach a wider audience and increase their chances of success.

Parents, too, can benefit from understanding algorithmic changes. As social media becomes an integral part of teenagers' lives, parents need to be aware of the platforms their children are using. By understanding algorithms, parents can guide their children to create content that aligns with their values while ensuring their safety and privacy online.

For fitness and wellness influencers, staying on top of algorithmic changes is vital to maintaining visibility and staying relevant. Algorithms often prioritize content that generates high engagement, so understanding how to optimize posts for maximum reach is crucial. This subchapter will delve into strategies such as utilizing trending hashtags, creating engaging captions, and posting at optimal times to maximize visibility and engagement with the target audience.

Adapting to changes in algorithms requires constant learning and experimentation. It is essential to monitor platform updates, follow industry experts, and engage with the community to stay informed. By embracing change and being flexible in your content creation approach, you can thrive in the ever-evolving world of social media.

In conclusion, whether you're a teenager, parent, or fitness and wellness influencer, understanding and adapting to changes in algorithms is essential for success in the social media game. This subchapter will equip you with the knowledge and strategies needed to navigate algorithmic changes, increase visibility, and maintain relevance in the online world. Stay tuned and get ready to master the art of influencing with the power of algorithmic adaptability.

Continuously Evolving as an Influencer

In this digital age, where social media platforms have become the new playground for self-expression and influence, being an influencer has become a coveted title. Whether you are a teenager looking to make your mark in the online world, a parent trying to understand your child's fascination with becoming an influencer, or a fitness and wellness enthusiast seeking to inspire others, this subchapter will guide you on the journey of continuously evolving as an influencer.

Being an influencer is not just about gaining followers or creating captivating content; it is a commitment to personal growth and constant improvement. As a teenager, it is crucial to remember that becoming an influencer is a process that requires time, dedication, and a willingness to learn. It is essential to find your passion and niche, whether it is fashion, beauty, gaming, or fitness, and consistently work on developing your skills and knowledge in that area.

Parents play a vital role in supporting their children's dreams of becoming influencers. It is important to understand that being an influencer goes beyond just a hobby; it can be a legitimate career path. Encouraging your child to explore their interests and providing them with guidance and resources to enhance their skills will help them in their journey. However, it is equally important to ensure that they maintain a healthy balance between their online presence and their personal lives.

For fitness and wellness influencers, the journey of continuously evolving revolves around staying up-to-date with the latest trends, research, and industry developments. Your audience expects you to provide them with valuable knowledge and insights. Therefore, it is crucial to invest time in self-education, attend workshops and seminars, and collaborate with experts in your field. Additionally, experimenting with different workout routines, nutrition plans, and wellness practices will help you provide fresh and diverse content to your followers.

In conclusion, being an influencer is a dynamic and ever-evolving process. Whether you are a teenager, parent, or fitness and wellness enthusiast, the key to success lies in continuously learning, adapting, and growing. Embrace the journey, be open to feedback, and never stop challenging yourself. Remember, as an influencer, you have the power to inspire and positively impact the lives of others. So, keep evolving, keep creating, and keep influencing!

Conclusion: Mastering the Social Media Game

Congratulations! By reading "The Art of Influence: Mastering the Social Media Game," you have taken the first step towards becoming a master of the ever-evolving world of social media. Whether you are a teenager, parent, or aspiring YouTuber, this book has provided you with valuable insights and strategies to navigate the digital landscape successfully. In this concluding chapter, we will summarize the key takeaways and offer some final words of advice to help you thrive in your chosen niche, whether it be as an influencer or a fitness and wellness influencer.

First and foremost, remember that social media is a powerful tool that can be used for both personal and professional purposes. As a teenager, it is crucial to understand the impact social media can have on your life. Use it wisely, exercise caution, and be mindful of the content you share. Parents, actively engage with your children, educate them about responsible social media use, and ensure they understand the potential consequences of their actions online.

For aspiring YouTubers and influencers, consistency and authenticity are key. Building a loyal following takes time and effort, so make sure to consistently create and share high-quality content that resonates with your target audience. Stay true to yourself and your passions, as authenticity is what will set you apart from others in the crowded social media landscape.

If you are interested in becoming a fitness and wellness influencer, prioritize your own health and well-being. Remember that your audience looks up to you as a role model, so it is essential to practice what you preach. Continuously educate yourself, stay up-to-date with the latest fitness trends and research, and always strive to provide accurate information and advice to your followers.

Lastly, do not underestimate the power of community. Social media is not just about self-promotion; it is about building relationships and fostering a sense of belonging. Engage with your audience, respond to comments and messages, and create a safe and inclusive space for your followers to interact with one another. Collaborate with other influencers in your niche, attend events, and network both online and offline. Remember, success on social media is not a solitary journey but a collective effort.

In conclusion, mastering the social media game requires dedication, authenticity, and a genuine desire to make a positive impact on others' lives. Whether you are a teenager, parent, or aspiring influencer in the fitness and wellness niche, the strategies outlined in this book will serve as a solid foundation for building your online presence. Embrace the opportunities that social media presents, but always remember to use it responsibly and ethically. Good luck on your journey, and may you become a true master of the social media game!

In today's digital age, social media has become an integral part of our lives. It has revolutionized the way we connect, communicate, and even influence others. Whether you're a teenager trying to navigate the complex world of social media, a parent concerned about your child's online presence, or a YouTuber looking to enhance your influence, this subchapter will provide valuable insights into the art of influence within the context of social media.

1. Understanding the Power of Influence
Influence is a powerful tool that can be harnessed for both positive and negative purposes. We will explore the concept of influence, how it works, and why it matters in the context of social media. By understanding the power of influence, teenagers can make informed decisions about the content they consume and parents can guide their children towards responsible online behavior.

2. Navigating the Social Media Landscape
Social media platforms are constantly evolving, and it's important to stay up-to-date with the latest trends and features. We will discuss the most popular platforms and provide tips for creating engaging content that resonates with your target audience. For YouTubers, we will delve into the strategies that can

help you grow your channel and increase your influence within the fitness and wellness niche.

3. Building a Personal Brand

In the world of social media, a strong personal brand is crucial for establishing credibility and attracting a loyal following. We will guide teenagers and YouTubers on how to define their personal brand, create a unique identity, and maintain authenticity in their content. Parents will gain insights into helping their children develop a positive online persona while maintaining their privacy and safety.

4. Leveraging Influence for Good

Influence can be a force for positive change. We will explore ways in which teenagers, parents, and YouTubers can use their influence to promote fitness and wellness, inspire others, and create a supportive online community. We will provide practical tips and examples of successful campaigns that have made a real impact.

Remember, the sub-chapter numbering used here is just for illustration purposes. Adjust it as per your book's content and structure. By mastering the art of influence on social media, teenagers, parents, and YouTubers can navigate the digital landscape with confidence, make a positive impact, and achieve their goals within the fitness and wellness influencer niche.